What people are saying about Tanii Carr's *Ten Weeks to Love:*

"Truly, a book that inspires hope! What you've done is unique, much needed and will help readers find the lasting and loving happiness they are seeking."

CARRIE KISH
CPCC Life Coach

"Tanii Carr's vibrant commitment to life and her true desire to help people are evident in this wonderful book. It is fun to read and is full of riveting, yet simple truths. I'm glad she decided to share her insights, as I know they will help a lot of people, myself included! This is a book you will cherish and want to share with others."

LEE KESSLER
Television actress, playwright, stage director
Author, the "White King" trilogy

"Yours is one of the best self-help books I've ever read! Not just on the subject of finding great love, but on any subject involving people and relationships. I read it cover to cover—couldn't put it down. If you want to help yourself and find your soul-mate, read *Ten Weeks to Love!*"

"BAD BOB" SALERNO
World champion ski legend
Co-Founder, Virtual Snow

"Amazing book and great read! So informative—I couldn't put it down!"

JANE GETZ
Songwriter, record producer, jazz artist

"In Tanii Carr's wonderful book, *Ten Weeks to Love*, you'll find not only great advice on finding true love, but advice on loving yourself and becoming your best you. The advice is sprinkled with a dose of humor, making the book a delight to read. By having the courage to share the ups and downs of her life, Tanii helps provide a path for others to find their own happiness."

DENISE BROWN
Entertainment industry attorney

"Tanii's insightful and delightful book wisely guides readers through the maze of finding big love. With her own great marriage, she sets a perfect example of how others can achieve their own happily-ever-afters."

KATHY OLIVER
Creative director/producer (film and television)

"I recently read *Ten Weeks to Love* by Tanii Carr. The first thing I loved was the subtitle: *How I Went From Divorced And Miserable To Happily Married Without Losing Weight, Having Plastic Surgery Or Being Completely Sane!* As someone who has owned and managed a dating service for over 25 years, I was intensely interested in what she had to say, and can heartily recommend this book to everyone I know who is single and looking."

MARCIA POWELL
Owner, Affinity Exchange

"Haven't found the love of your life yet? You just may, now that you found this book! Tanii Carr's intelligent, funny, step-by-step account of how she manifested the love of her life offers a concise, no-nonsense, get-your-ass-in-gear game plan for finding your soul-mate that is waiting to be discovered. But a word of WARNING: Read this book at the risk of losing any excuses you may still have for not accomplishing your romantic goals."

MARK OMAN
Bestselling golf humorist, columnist, and motivational speaker
(…and beloved brother of author, Tanii Carr!)

"All I can say is WOW! What a clear, interesting and honest way of laying out how people, male or female, can accomplish what they want in matters of the heart or in life itself!"

PEGGY POE
Educator

"Your book is well written and provided me with insight into why you and Charles are such a special couple. I loved you before reading your wonderful book, but even more so now, with respect and admiration for your honesty toward helping others achieve the great loves they seek."

AVERY KAY
Colonel, USAF (retired),
Veteran (WWII, Korea, Vietnam), NATO

TEN WEEKS TO *Love*

How I Went From Divorced and Miserable to Happily Married Without Losing Weight, Having Plastic Surgery or Being Completely Sane!

A Book of Hope and Help

by

TANII CARR

Wedding invitation, February, 1987

For further information, contact the author directly through her website: www.10weeks2love.com

Library of Congress Cataloging-in-Publication Data is available upon request.

ISBN 978-0-9892588-1-4

This book is dedicated to my amazing and
wonderful husband, Charles A. Carr.
Without him, there would be no story to tell,
no book to write.

Tanii Carr,
Shadow Hills, CA

CONTENTS

PREFACE

*I*T WAS SATURDAY, JANUARY 31ST. ALL I WANTED HIM TO *do was help me load a heavy chair from my garage into a borrowed truck. Simple. I was 45; he had just* turned 29 (yes, 29). The following Friday we decided to get married and did so three weeks later, exactly four weeks after that fateful Saturday when my life changed forever.

On February 28, 2013, we celebrated our 26th anniversary. He still thinks I'm eye candy and I still think he's the sexiest, most amazing man I've ever known.

I know exactly what I did to go from twice-divorced and miserable to meeting the man of my dreams in a few short weeks. What I did is the subject of this book, *Ten Weeks to Love*.

I hope my love story will inspire you to create one of your own.

(Note: In case you are already champing at the bit to get started, be patient for just a bit longer—long enough to get through my Introduction—as there are some key instructions and insights which you may find useful as you read on!)

Mother, bless her heart, wanted to help. But she was more of a mess than I was, even if I didn't think so at the time. Beneath the obvious glamour, she was beautiful on the inside—well-read and for as long as I can remember, searching for the answers to existence itself.

INTRODUCTION

OST OF MY ADULT LIFE WAS SPENT IN THE PURSUIT OF A *romantic dream that had somehow eluded me except in brief. There was nothing really wrong with me, but no* amount of compliments to the contrary from friends and family could convince me otherwise. The fact that I could not for the life of me figure out how to have a successful, happy, and lasting relationship convinced me that I was seriously and irreparably flawed. As far as I was concerned, I was hopeless.

MOTHER

Mother, bless her heart, wanted to help. But she was more of a mess than I was, even if I didn't think so at the time. In fact, she was married so many times that to this day my brother and I still cannot agree on how many times she was married and to whom (although we do estimate that number to be between six and ten, including the two times she married and divorced Dad). We laugh about it, but it's a pretty sad commentary on a life very much spent in the pursuit of happiness and finding it only fleetingly at best.

The fact that she was glamorous and gorgeous didn't help my self-esteem either, especially when I was a teenager. Mother had been a model, showgirl, and actress. Honestly, when she got dressed up, she could stop traffic! As a young girl, I thought she was everything I wanted to be: tall, gorgeous, charming, and funny. But mostly I wanted to get the attention that she always got from men. I thought she was happy, because I would have been happy to have been so blessed, or so I thought at the time.

Puberty changed all

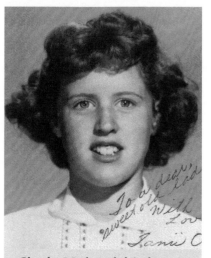

Clearly Mother didn't love me very much as evidenced by the fact that she let me go out in public with that hair! Kidding aside, she was generous. We didn't have much money at the time, so when I couldn't afford a new pair of shoes, she let me wear her very stylish black flats to school. They were too big for me, so I stuffed the toes with tissue. I walked funny because the shoes kept coming off, but I was happy.

that. Boys started hanging around, but it soon became clear that they were there to be with Mother, not me. In retrospect, I know she didn't intend to hurt me, but her own insecurities compelled her to seek attention wherever she could, even if that happened to be at my expense. All I saw at the time was that compared to her, I was plain and undesirable. I was certain that I was never going to be able to compete. Had I been able to see beyond my own hurt, I would have known how unhappy and unfulfilled she was and perhaps felt better about myself and my chances for happiness.

MARRIAGE #1

My first marriage was brief. I ended it. I had unexpressed misgivings even as my intended and I walked down the aisle. I was too cowardly to speak up before the "I dos." Had I done so, I could have saved my fiancé, his family and everyone involved a great deal of upset.

MARRIAGE #2

My second marriage lasted seven and a half years, which was seven and a half years—minus one day—longer than it should have. When your husband of one day says that he thinks maybe it was a mistake to have gotten married, the *wrong* thing to do is to wonder what <u>you</u> did wrong, and then spend the next several years trying to make it right.

What I should have done was to thank him for his honesty, tell him he had 24 hours to sort it out, and in the meantime, he could sleep on the couch.

Much as I didn't appreciate some of his actions during our marriage—actions consistent with someone who was unhappy in that marriage—I had to admit that blaming him never really made me feel better or bring me closer to understanding what happened, let alone closer to the fulfilling relationship I said I wanted.

And while complaining to friends brought temporary comfort—friends tend to sympathize and make you right about your viewpoint—I still wasn't getting any closer to turning things around.

After Husband No. 2 and I parted company, things were tough even if the break-up was ultimately the best thing that could have happened to me. And then there was the fear that things might get worse. After all, I wasn't getting any younger and according to some popular women's magazines, my chances for romance were dwindling with age and the effects of gravity on the body.

●

Shortly after Charley and I got married, several people were referred to me by mutual friends who knew the saga of Charley and me getting together. I knew then, as I recount now, exactly what I did to do my part in bringing us together and was happy to share that information.

I wish that I had kept track of all those people and could share their stories with you. However, I do vividly recall the situation in which one young lady found herself. She was a student, living in an apartment building with other students. She had a boyfriend. She wanted to get married; he made it clear he did not. He asked her to move in with him. Her thinking was that if she moved in, despite his avowed disinterest in tying the knot, he would come to realize her value and want to marry her.

I told her some of the things that I had done that led to me and Charley getting together, especially on the matter of sticking to one's integrity as regards goals and purposes. I encouraged her to follow the path that would more certainly lead to what she ultimately wanted. I felt that she knew, deep down, what the right choice was even if it was tough to admit to it.

While I did give her some ideas to think about, I felt it was important for her to solve the problem for herself, rather than me telling her what to do. Though the decision she made was ultimately of her own choosing—the result of her own inspection of the facts which only she, having firsthand knowledge, would know—I did feel strongly that the odds of this guy changing because she moved in with him were slim to none.

A few weeks later she called to tell me what happened following our conversation. Though it was hard for her to do, she called the boyfriend and told him that since she was after something different in a relationship than he was, it was better if they broke it off and go their separate ways. She followed up with a call to a girlfriend, letting her know what had happened. When she got off the phone with the girlfriend, a fellow student living in the building came over to her and told her that he couldn't help hearing part of her conversation with her friend—particularly the part about breaking off the relationship with the boyfriend.

He proceeded to tell her that he had been smitten with her since the first time he had seen her, but felt it would be inappropriate to try to muscle in given that she was in a relationship. But, now that she had broken if off, would she like to have dinner with him? Well, dinner led to more dinners, which led to getting married within the following two months!

●

TRANSFORMATION!

I'm happy to report, however, that I beat the odds. I did climb out of the hole I had so creatively dug for myself. I did find someone about whom I was excited and who was just as excited about me. I did get married, and after 26 years, still think that I'm the luckiest woman in the world to be married to this extraordinary man.

WHO AM I TO GIVE ADVICE?

My transformation from stupid and miserable "dumpee" to happy, confident and loved woman took a surprisingly short amount of time (a few weeks). Over the years I had considered writing it all down, but I wanted to make sure that the relationship would last before passing myself off as some expert. I wanted to be a real-life example of what I was advising.

That said, I figure that 26 years of a great marriage and relationship gives me some real-life credentials. I didn't get it right for a long time—like a lot of folks. I've been in the trenches—like a lot of folks. But I finally did get it right— like I hope a lot of folks will do from reading this book!

COURAGE TO ACT!

This is not some lofty volume on theories of love. It is at least as much about things to do as it is about things to think about—less thinking, more action.

The things I learned through my own experiences led to some amazingly simple truths. But as simple as these truths ultimately are, it takes a commitment, persistence and no small amount of courage to face the lies we've told ourselves—or bought into from others—along the way.

MY PROBLEMS, MY SOLUTIONS

The steps I took in creating a better life for myself grew out of my circumstances and my problems. Though I hope you will read the whole book and accompanying exercises, not everything I did will necessarily be relevant to you and your situation.

Ultimately, it's about improving conditions. If a chapter or exercise doesn't seem to apply to your life at the moment, go on to the next chapter and set of exercises. You can always come back to that material at a later time.

MEN?

Though this book was written from the obvious perspective of a woman of a certain age and life experience, my story and loss and fulfillment could just as easily be that of a man. Love, loss, pain, sorrow, happiness, fulfillment, dreams, enthusiasm are equal-opportunity emotions and experiences. Ultimately, we are individuals—beings—first, men and women second.

RELEVANCE

I originally thought that my story would only be of interest or relevance to mature women who'd been divorced or otherwise had lost at love. And I certainly wanted to give them hope that despite prior failures, there was still a chance for them to find the person of their dreams.

But every time I told my story (the brief version as it appears in my Preface), the immediate response was, "Where can I buy the book?!" This response was coming from people of all ages, socio-economic groups, single or divorced, men and women—this was the uniform response!

That said, I recently was discussing my book with a very intelligent professional gentleman who, while interested in the subject matter, played Devil's Advocate long enough to question the relevance of my story to today's mass audience. "Yes, you have an enviable life, but your story is 26 years old. Isn't it a bit *outdated*? What can you tell us that is trendier and more timely?"

The comment caused me to seriously consider his point of view. Was I wasting my time writing a book or trying to help others if no one will find inspiration in its pages or take inspiration from my 26-year-old story?

But the responses I've been getting—and the statistics on relationships—don't lie. Divorce continues to plague way too many couples. Single-parenthood is still a fact of modern life. Young people, perhaps because of what they see in their parents or others, are increasingly opting for non-marital relationships over marriage.

Because our traditional notions about what marriage is have changed so much over these many years, there seems to be more confusion than ever about what will work and what won't work, or if marriage itself is outmoded. Can marriage survive modern times?

Keep in mind that all these dreadful statistics and conditions exist at a time when the number of books, blogs, CDs, magazine articles (online and off), seminars, coaching—and professionals out there writing, lecturing, and trying to help—are at an all-time high due to our ever-present access to information through the Internet!

Clearly, people are still looking for answers!

What, therefore, could be more "timely" than two people who have weathered these changes and challenges, who continue to be glad they got married, who are increasingly happy as individuals and fulfilling their individual and collective goals? What could be more relevant than finding hope in their example?

Love is always relevant. And until the day when divorce is a rarity, and more children grow up in loving homes with thoughtful and happy parents, information on how to find love and meaningful coexistence will continue to be sought after and relevant.

MISERABLE VS HAPPY

Frankly, I'm tired of seeing people miserable, confused, frustrated, bewildered, and sad when they could be confident, happy, fulfilled, and enjoying life. And while I can't promise that by reading this book, the sky will suddenly open up and Mr. or Ms. Right will drop from the heavens, I can tell you that to the degree you take back ownership for the condition your love life is in, clear out the old and formerly uninspected ideas, viewpoints, and games that haven't worked, and maintain your personal integrity (you may have to find it again), you can dramatically improve your chances of finding the love and relationship you've been searching for.

It's okay if you happen to be gorgeous, handsome, or super-model thin…but you don't have to be. You don't have to be debt-free, rich, or super-intelligent. You can do it if you've never been married, if you've been married before and failed at it, or if you have kids that you think no one else will want. You can do it even it you don't go to parties or bars, or hang out at singles' clubs. In fact, I firmly believe that even if you were in a town where your sex outnumbered the opposite sex, you'd still pull it off, unless, of course, everybody else was reading my book too!

I wish I could have shared this information with Mom, who died way too young never knowing how great life could be with the right person. Perhaps I can help offset her loss by helping others.

Empiezo (Empy) was my dream horse, or so I imagined. He was gorgeous, talented, a national champion and sweet when we first met—all things (and more) that I had named on my dream-horse wish list. And then he attacked me, leaving me bruised and dismayed with a devastating blow to my confidence. It was hard to face the facts, but in the year that preceded the attack, he had displayed increasingly dominant behavior which I was not handling well. I had been wrong in my choice of a horse-mate and just couldn't admit it—or deal with it—pretty much like my second marriage. (Note: I found Empy a great home with a talented and gifted horsewoman. Unlike him and me, they are a great match!)

OH MISERY, THOU NAME BE DIVORCE!

*M*Y SECOND DIVORCE LEFT ME A BIT SHELL-SHOCKED *and reeling from the frustrations and embarrassment of the failure of yet another marriage—all of the "I should have knowns" that I didn't know. (Actually,* that's not a true statement. Deep down I did know; I just lacked the courage to act on what I knew.)

After the reality sank in that there would be no reconciliation (he left me for another woman and was planning to marry her when the divorce was final), I began to look toward the future, which, at the time, looked pretty bleak. I knew generally what I wanted—and specifically what I didn't want! In my head I was already working on my wish list, my romantic Vision Statement. (On more than one occasion over the years, I had written what seemed like volumes on "my ideal man" without the hoped-for outcome. As part of the process outlined in this book, I will share with you what I discovered as to why such exercises often fail and what needs to be in place first to make them work.)

WANTING . . .

I knew, for one thing, that I wanted to be with someone who wanted to be with me with equal enthusiasm. In my first marriage, my husband wanted to create the relationship more than I did. And in the second marriage, it was just the opposite. Not good either way, and definitely no fun.

I knew I wanted to experience happiness, even if I didn't know exactly what that meant. And that I didn't want to feel that I had to act like someone else in order to satisfy the relationship. Frankly, it's a lot of work to try to be someone you're not.

I wanted someone I could talk to—someone who would be my best friend, and vice versa. I wanted the relationship to be fun, light, and lively. I didn't want to spend my waking hours worrying about what things I might say that would upset my husband, or to be overly thankful for bits of affection occasionally tossed my way. I didn't want to have to get angry to get a response because that almost always meant I had let my emotions go unexpressed for too long a time until they erupted all at once which was very stressful.

I wanted a good father figure for my son Josh, and I certainly did not want to put him through any more negative scenes. And I wanted a relationship wherein both of us would grow, and by being together, accomplish individual and mutual goals better than if we were not together.

While the details were formulating in my mind, I didn't expect some fancied perfection, because life just isn't that perfect. But I did very much want a marriage where this person and I had a better-than-even chance of making it over time, where the major goals were agreed upon (even if some of the smaller ones were not), and where there was enough agreement, respect, and affection that it was worth working out the inevitable stresses that would surely come up.

Mostly I wanted to improve my chances for happiness, even though at the time I wasn't sure what exactly I should look for in a prospective mate. (I thought I had done that with the last husband. Clearly something was not right about my approach.)

...BUT NOT GETTING!

Well, this all sounded pretty good to me in these conversations with myself. I was an intelligent person. In the past, when I wanted something—really wanted it—I'd figure out how to get it and then, well, just get it! But here was this area where I kept saying, *I want a relationship. I want to get married again. I want someone in my life*...but nothing was happening—nada, zip, zero!

I also knew from prior experience in other areas of my life, that if I repeatedly said I wanted something and wasn't getting it, that the reasons for failure were *internal*, not external. In this case, it was just plain illogical to suppose that with all the millions of people on this planet, I couldn't find *anyone* to suit my needs. It just wasn't logical. (I struggled with this "logic" elsewhere in my journey. See Chapter Nine for more on this subject.)

Okay. So the first thing that I had to get my wits around was that if I SAID I wanted a great guy and great relationship, but didn't HAVE that kind of guy or relationship, there must be one or more reasons, unknown or hidden, that were keeping me from having the things I said I wanted. But what could they be?

It has been said often and in various ways that as a man thinketh, so he is. We'd like to think that our thoughts, ideas, or concepts about life are arrived at after careful and deliberate examination and analysis. But the truth is that some thoughts or ideas are just as likely, or more likely, to be acquired from other people without inspection— considerations and decisions about life and love that bind us to and dictate actions that are more *reactive* (knee-jerk responses to earlier situations or problems) than analytical. Either way—and for better or worse—our thoughts precede and are the stuff of which we create our lives, our futures. In fact, these uninspected decisions and choices that are the worst, because they trap us and we don't know it!

So I reasoned that I'd better look really hard to see if I had any thoughts, opinions, or ideas—or had drawn any conclusions based on these thoughts, opinions, ideas, or experiences—that could be counter-productive to achieving my relationship goals. (How about the one that tells you there aren't any good men or women left? Now there's a decision that will kill a relationship before it even starts!)

A FRESH LOOK AT RELATIONSHIPS

The exercise I devised to ferret out these uninspected decisions involved writing down all the reasons why it would NOT be such a good idea to get involved with someone—why it *wouldn't* be good to fall in love or get married again.

When I actually sat down and made my list, I was absolutely amazed at all the mental blocks I had placed across my own path! Some thoughts made sense, sort of. For example, I didn't want to fail again; if a relationship turned out badly, I would be unhappy and I didn't want to be unhappy again. These ideas were understandable, but still represented a reaction to one or more earlier experiences. And the worry that I felt under the surface was not very productive as it contained an element of fear, the origins of which I did not understand, but nonetheless experienced.

One of the first big mental blocks that I felt I really had to face and resolve—because it was so all-encompassing— was the question as to whether any relationship, even a good one, was worth the effort—in other words, if the pain/pleasure ratio was too heavily weighted on the side of pain.

At that point in my life, I had serious misgivings about the value of relationships generally. "Experience" had "taught me" that perhaps this was an area to steer clear of…permanently. Isn't it better, after all, to be by oneself and be reasonably happy, than to be in a bad relationship and be miserable? While I do believe the answer is *yes*, that seemingly rational thought had migrated over into "relationships are bad." And yet I still longed for a relationship!

What a mental tug-o-war! What subconscious stress! So long as these two thoughts were in opposition to each other, there was no solution! *I want it, but I don't want it, but I do want it…* Push, pull, push, pull. Yes, no, yes, no. Maybe!

Once I recognized this mental conflict was undermining my forward progress, I set about evaluating the pros and cons of being in a relationship at all. How? By looking around at couples I knew, or knew about, in search of those that appeared to be happy. (I already knew what unhappy couples looked like—they looked like me and my exes—so I didn't need to inspect them.)

I talked to people I knew, observed others, and read magazine articles about couples that seemed to have their lives together. What were their lives like? Were they doing better together than they had been before they got together? Did those relationships enhance their lives or detract from them? Did they appear happy and fulfilled in those relationships or was it all pretense?

DECISION!

I did a lot of looking and applied myself to the task as one might research a less-emotionally-involving subject. And what all this "homework" told me was that the happier couples that I admired seemed to have more of their lives together than the unhappy ones. They certainly didn't act as though they had given up their individual selves in order to satisfy their partners. In fact, their individual strengths seemed to contribute to the success of their relationships, and through those relationships they became stronger as individuals.

Though I still had doubts about my own ability to achieve such a relationship, it was now clear to me that a good relationship had merit and was worth having. Albeit cautiously, I felt it was okay to proceed.

Chapter One Exercises

1a Make a list of all the reasons it might NOT be a good idea to be in a relationship.

1b For each item listed, write down how you arrived at that thought, idea, or conclusion.

- Did some "friend" warn you "for your own good?"
- Did you read it in some magazine?
- Did you decide this was true because of some bad experience?
- Did you arrive at this conclusion because your parents were miserable?
- What?

1c Now, with the dispassion of a research scientist—unemotional and personally uninvolved—examine each of the above reasons to see if they are, in fact, valid.

- Do they apply to your life as it is in the present, or did they apply to an earlier time or set of circumstances?
- Did that reason or reasons apply across the boards or could one find examples to support a different conclusion?
- Do you need to look at other people to see if your thoughts on the subject are the only thoughts possible?

- Does your previous thought on the subject solve the problem and leave you feeling good about the subject or does it contribute to stress?

2a Look around at couples who appear to be happy and in successful relationships.

- Do they have relationships you think you'd like to have?
- Do they seem to enjoy life or do they complain a lot and are difficult to be around?
- Do both partners appear to be happy with each other and their lives?
- Are they people you enjoy having as friends or would like to have as friends?
- Do they have fun and are they nice people, or are they self-centered, dull, or manifest negative emotions?

The hoped-for end result of this exercise is a decision about relationships generally—they are either a good thing worth pursuing, or not—a fresh look at the subject, based on the facts and circumstances of your life, your goals, your priorities. No more doubts or reservations, either way.

If you decide that relationships are a good thing, terrific! Proceed!

If you decide that relationships are <u>not</u> for you—and feel good about that decision—by God, stick with that choice, without apology knowing that it is the right decision for you and your life and a choice you arrived at by personal inspection and self-determinism.

If, however, you still are unsure on this subject, keep looking for examples until you've seen enough to be able to weigh the pros and cons. You also might try prioritizing the issues on which your decision will be based. For example, it may be **really important** to you that you both share the same religion, so that "issue" might have more value and weight (a rating of 10) in arriving at a conclusion than another, less important issue (a rating of 3).

While I personally have come to believe that a relationship of the heart can enhance anyone's life, I am willing to concede that under certain circumstances, it may not be workable.

At the very least, this exercise should help give you more clarity as to which conclusion has more happiness and meaning associated with it.

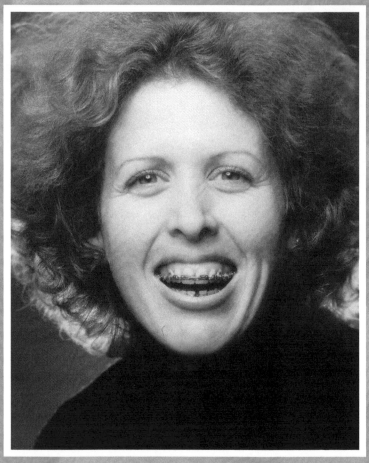

This publicity shot got me a part in the movie The Rabbit Test, Joan Rivers first directorial effort. Most actors worry that even though they got paid, their parts might get cut from the movie they were in. As it turned out, the two scenes I was in were the two scenes Joan used to promote the movie all across the U.S.! It wasn't because I was so good, it was because Billy Crystal was in those scenes and they were funny. It was daring to wear a mouth full of metal while working for a major television station. But improving my smile could not compensate for the confusion and mental blocks keeping me from attracting the great love I hoped was out there—at least not then.

BEFORE MENTAL BLOCKS

*O*THER MENTAL BOOBY TRAPS, WHILE APPEARING *logical to me at the time, were real head-scratchers. For example, I didn't want to bring any debts to a new relationship. I had a lot of debts from my* previous marriage. It was going to take me a long time to pay them off and I just believed it would be inconsiderate of me to bring my financial problems to a new relationship. Makes sense, right?

NO! NO! I'M NOT READY YET!

So here was this idea: *I have to pay off my debts before getting into a new relationship.* Okay, fine. Except that this idea, all by itself, could sabotage or at least seriously delay my goal of finding someone with whom to share my life. This particular issue definitely thwarted my forward progress and was not necessarily relevant.

Another decision I had made was that I needed to be wiser and more intelligent on the subject of business, because I was <u>certain</u> that one reason my second marriage had failed was because I wasn't good at the businesses in which my ex-husband and I were involved. But that, too, could take time, putting off even further the dream I longed to make reality before my 80th birthday!

I wanted to lose 15 pounds and be more physically fit. But since my life at the time was consumed with finding work and getting back on track as a matter of basic survival, that wasn't a very realistic goal to accomplish in a reasonably short period of time.

Here are a few more of the other "I'll-be-ready-for-a-great-guy-when _____ *(fill in the blank)* has-been-handled" kind of mental blocks:

- When I've sorted out my career path
- When I'm successful in business
- When I'm a better cook
- When I'm a better lover
- When my head is more together

There were other "before" issues, but at the time, I was certain that if those things were in place, there was no way that I could fail at another relationship. Why? Because at that time I was convinced that my failure at these things was the real reason the earlier marriages had bombed. *If only I could change these terrible things about myself, all would be well.*

So I made another list, this time of all those things that I felt had to be done *before* I could or should embark on a new relationship. And from this list, I began to see just how critical of myself I had become.

(Blaming myself, by the way, never led to any recognition of the real reasons behind my failures. Self-blame did, however, serve a purpose in providing me with a somewhat comfortable place to emotionally park while getting up the courage to take real responsibility and ownership for my part in the demise of those marriages. *Blame* was a passive activity and required no particular effort on my part. In fact it was pretty easy. *Responsibility* was going to take <u>action</u> and <u>participation</u> and I hadn't been there for awhile.)

ONLY THE GOOD STUFF!

On a visit to see my doctor, I told his wife about what I was running into—including all the self-blame. Mercifully, she cut me off after a few minutes to give me an assignment: I was to write down all the reasons why someone would find me desirable as a girlfriend or wife. I was not *allowed* to write anything negative—no inadequacies whatever— just good and positive things about myself.

At first, it was extremely difficult. During the course of my second marriage, I had progressively thought less and less of myself, so this was surprisingly difficult...at first. *Well, I'm nice,* I wrote. Minutes passed. *I'm cheerful...most of the time.* More minutes—but not as many—passed. *I have a good sense of humor.* Hmm, that felt good. *I'm* (dare I commit to paper?)*...attractive! And I'm intelligent...and honest...and...and...and.* Pretty soon compliments were pouring forth with great speed! And by the time I was done, I had written three pages of qualities that would make me desirable as a mate! (Thanks Isela!)

The scales were shifting! I had a lot to recommend me even if I still had debts and an extra 15 pounds. Self-loathing was down; confidence was on the rise. Things were looking up!

Additionally, by now having a more balanced view of myself, I could reinspect the list of things-that-must-be-done-before-I-can-pursue-a-relationship and decide, with greater perspective and clarity, whether the items on the list were valid concerns or unimportant as prerequisites to love. Ultimately, most items on the list were rejected as prerequisites, even if they remained as goals.

•

As an aside, in case any of you are interested, what I later discovered as the real reason I had put up with a less-than-desirable marriage had little or nothing to do with the subject of personal relationships. It had to do with my unwillingness to enter the workforce again and my lack of confidence in earlier career choices. In retrospect, it seems ridiculous and stupid, but at the time it seemed easier to face what was becoming predictable misery at home than to face the prospect of being unpredictably miserable in work. At least for a time I felt more comfortable with the routine of being unhappy than the uncertainty of professional failure. Basically, I was hiding out in a bad marriage—poor pitiful me! Of course, the problem I couldn't face before the marriage was still there after the marriage broke up, only compounded by more problems. However, its eventual discovery was wonderfully freeing and part of my journey, therefore part of my growth.

●

OUR LITTLE JOKE

Over the years, when asked about the story of how Charley and I got together—and our age difference—I told people that the *actual* reason I spent all those years getting married and divorced twice, was because I had to bide my time waiting for Charley to turn 18. Which led to other silly comments about the fact that with the 16-year spread in our respective ages, I could have been his babysitter. Notwithstanding his future status as my husband, it would have been highly inappropriate for me to look at this toddler in diapers and be thinking "husband material?"

Funny, weird and creepy all at the same time.

Okay, let's move on.

CHAPTER TWO EXERCISES

1a. Make a list of everything you feel needs to be done before you should, could, or deserve to have a new and wonderful relationship.

1b. Review each item and decide if it really needs to be done beforehand or not. For any that do <u>not</u> need to be done first, cross them off the list.

1c. For items you truly and validly believe MUST be done before embarking on a new relationship (like getting a divorce before you take up with someone else—hello!), make a simple and realistic plan for resolving that issue including an estimation of the amount of time that will be involved. If this plan becomes too lengthy or complicated, inspect the item again to make sure that there isn't something you haven't looked at as to why it absolutely MUST be done before you can pursue your goal of having a new relationship.

At the end of this exercise, and as you put order into your life, you should start to feel more at ease and more relaxed. Maybe you walk a little taller and feel more confident in your ability to be in control. You might even start to look a little better and more refreshed because all the worry you've been carrying around takes a toll on you—physically, emotionally, and spiritually—and it eventually shows on your face and in your eyes. And in matters of the heart, you want to look your best!

2a. List all the reasons why someone would find you attractive and desirable as a mate. No negatives allowed on this list!! Don't even go there! Odds are, you've been beating yourself up over what's wrong with you already. You don't need a list for that! You've probably been carrying one around in your head for way too long!

You can certainly add to this list any time you want to, but you're done with it when you feel really good about yourself as a romantic prospect—not just "Yeah, I guess I'm okay…" No! You are done with this exercise when you can see that your positive attributes and goodness in the romance department OUTWEIGH any negatives that you might bring to a relationship. When you know, from all the evidence that you've amassed on your list, that you would be an ASSET to any good relationship, not a LIABILITY, then you can consider that this exercise is DONE!

Not all games are created equal. Though they have the same components—goals, barriers, rules, teams and teammates—some are fun to play and some are not. Since Charley and I have been together, we've been able to play more of the fun kind. This picture was taken at our ranch in Placerita Canyon where Charley indulged me in my passion for horses. This is a much better game for me than the destructive ones I had sometimes played when looking for love.

GAMES PEOPLE PLAY

*T*HERE WAS, FOR ME, ANOTHER SET OF MENTAL *stumbling blocks to overcome.* * *And these had to do with silly but compelling games that were pretty much running on automatic pilot without my* conscious control. I'm not talking about games of choice that bring one pleasure and that one decides to play after thoughtful consideration. I'm talking about negative games, the reasons for playing such having been long since forgotten—games that control one's life without the individual knowing it.

As part of my exercise to identify and resolve formerly hidden mental stumbling blocks and self-created, self-perpetuated problems, I became aware of a destructive game I had played for a long time but had not previously recognized as such.

MY OWN WORST ENEMY

Over the years, I had had a string of men friends who were brilliant and handsome, but difficult and hard to deal with. Basically, they were trouble. These relationships always ended badly, which didn't keep me from dashing off to find another difficult guy!

Because I had a knack for dealing with such men—to a point—there was an element of dubious success, of winning, as if some elaborate contest was in progress.

It was in one such relationship with a talented if difficult man that I overheard myself saying to myself, *Wow! You are quite a woman Tanii. Those other women couldn't handle him, but you can!*

I was so proud and so self-absorbed…until I realized that without the "difficult man" part, no <u>victory</u> was possible. A good, sane guy = no win for this gal! Good, sane, nice guy = loss—at least in the context of that game! It is tantamount to a race in which the track is strewn with shards of glass and the victor is the guy who crosses the finish line with the most blood on his feet.

I mean, really! I was actively contributing to my own demise and somehow happy about it at the same time! And there was the evidence right in front of me. None of these relationships lasted. All ended in failure. To win was to lose. And any game with a guaranteed loss is not a game worth playing. And if you doubt that, you really need to look again.

The identification of this game and how it was negatively affecting me allowed me to have more control as to my romantic destiny. I could play the game or not, but now the power of choice was mine. And that is very empowering! In the end—and with my new resolve to have a happier life—I elected to ditch the old game and find a new one at which I could win for real.

(*By definition, the act of *stumbling* is about things that are uncoordinated, awkward, unbalanced, clumsy, ungraceful, lacking control, and generally unattractive. Life poses plenty of real challenges that require control and grace under pressure. It is not particularly helpful to look or feel awkward, clumsy...and all those other words... about things which can be brought under one's own control if identified. Stumbling blocks do not enhance an individual's life; they are distractions.)

Chapter Three Exercises

1a. Look at your life to see if there is a *pattern* that you've manifested that has resulted in losses or failures in personal relationships—especially if this pattern has pretty much been running on automatic without your full causation and control.

1b. See if you can identify the specifics of the "game."

- When does it "kick in?" What happens just before?
- Who are the players?
- What is the anticipated outcome, good or bad?
- Does it involve opposition?
- What personality traits (other than your own) do you have to take on in order to "effectively" play this game?
- Does winning the game in some way result in losing—personal integrity, health, happiness, dignity?
- Is there some decision associated with this game? (Women only want me because I'm rich, so of course they'll betray me. Hmmmm.)

Now, with a fresh perspective, evaluate the merits of this former game (or games) and decide whether or not it brings you closer to your new goals for a happy and lasting relationship, or if in fact it sends you hurtling in the opposite direction. *The choice is yours!*

It took some doing for these two to get together—what with Eve living in Vienna, her family in Slovakia, and Josh living in the U.S. Josh is my son and Eve my wonderful daughter-in-law. They've been a great team. I love that they're part of the family!

DESPERATE OR DETERMINED?

I DON'T RECALL WHERE IN THE OVERALL PROCESS IT OCCURRED, BUT AT SOME *point—despite having renewed confidence that I had many desirable qualities—I had a screaming match with* myself in my car one night as I was driving down the Ventura Freeway near Los Angeles.

I mean yelling! At the top of my lungs! And crying! (Thankfully, it was dark so no one really saw or heard me.)

I was angry, not necessarily with or at myself, but just **angry** and telling myself, in no uncertain terms, that I simply HAD TO HANDLE this area, PERIOD!

That's it! You've got to handle this! And NOW! I'm tired of going home to an empty apartment! I'm tired of being the only one conducting my life! I'd like some help!!

For me, this increased demand was part of my new resolve to get what I wanted and what I increasingly believed I could actually get. The good news was that I was no longer apathetic. I no longer felt sorry for myself.

Rarely did I succumb to tears. Bit by bit, I was putting my life back in order and, by God, I was going to have what I wanted!

I think at some point, no matter the subject at hand, great strides or accomplishments are begun and achieved with a no-holds-barred attitude on the goal at hand. "Take no prisoners!" "Full speed ahead!" "Do or die!" are all attitudes that drive accomplishment. The following quote is one of my favorites and one to which I often refer:

> "Until one is committed there is hesitancy, the chance to draw back, always ineffectiveness. Concerning all acts of initiative (and creation), there is one elementary truth, the ignorance of which kills countless ideas and splendid plans: that the moment one definitely commits oneself, then Providence moves too. All sorts of things occur to help one that would never otherwise have occurred. A whole stream of events issues from the decision, raising in one's favor all manner of unforeseen incidents and meetings and material assistance, which no man could have dreamt would have come his way. I have learned a deep respect for one of Goethe's couplets: 'Whatever you can do or dream you can, begin it. Boldness has genius, power, and magic in it.'"
>
> W. H. Murray,
> The Second Himalayan Expedition

But this brings up another issue: When someone displays such strong intentions, are we looking at *determination* or *desperation*? What is the motivation behind such a strong desire? I definitely associate <u>determination</u> with things that are positive and <u>desperation</u> with things that are negative.

POPULARITY CONTESTS

When I was in junior and senior high school, I remember trying to figure out why the popular kids were popular, and why they never seemed to have problems getting dates (unlike moi).

It took many years before I realized that part of their attractiveness to others was that they *weren't desperate* for boyfriends or girlfriends. They seemed to be able to take it or leave it—dating and going steady.

I was beginning to see that this was a large part of being in a relationship. One was not *desperate,* because desperation was a sign that one was not confident, and no one who is him- or herself confident really wants to be with someone who isn't.

Further, when people are desperate they may do stupid, silly, and irrational things. They may try to be the thing or person they believe would make them more attractive to the object of their desires. They may become jealous and demanding. They may cease being themselves and in so doing, lose their personal integrity.

I saw myself in high school being on the desperate side of things with the predictable outcome. Or some boy was desperate to get close to me that I didn't like. No matter how I tried I just couldn't figure out how to have that "take it or leave it" attitude with the boys I liked! It was quite maddening.

(By the way, I think being a teenager is very rough on kids. My hat's off to parents who are grounded, caring, loving, firm when needed, and sane, because it takes a lot of patience, savvy and a great sense of humor to help kids get through what can be a most confusing time.)

Ultimately, I figured out how to achieve a measure of determination without the desperation part (read the next chapter), but the mere fact that I could now recognize the differences, manifestations, and effects created by those two attitudes was very helpful and allowed me to move one step closer to realizing my dreams.

Chapter Four Exercises

1a. Pick an area of your life—other than your love life—about which you feel confident.

1b. Was there ever a time when you *didn't* feel confident in this area? If so, what did you do to become confident?

1c. What things contributed to your confidence?

- Did those things involve learning something new?
- Did you gain confidence through others who knew more than you?
- How did you overcome moments of self-doubt?
- Did you have mentors—people who believed in you?
- Did you get the naysayers out of your life?

2. See if you can apply the successful actions learned in the above area to the subject of relationships.

- Do you surround yourself with people who believe in you and who support your desire to improve your love life?
- Have you been following the wrong "love gurus?"
- Is there anything you need to learn?
- Anything else that you can apply here?

3a. If you feel at all desperate about finding love, what are you worried about?

- What is the "awful" thing that will happen if you fail?
- Is there some other "horrible" thing you think will happen to you if you don't find your perfect mate?
- Keep adding to the list of awful, terrible, impossible-to-live-with eventualities that might befall you if Mr. or Ms. Right doesn't fall all over him- or herself to be by your side forever and ever.

3b. Rate each of the items on your list as to importance when compared to other areas of your life. For example, if you're worried and desperate about being lonely, how does that problem rate compared to losing your job?

3c. How could that problem be resolved other than worrying or being desperate about it? If you failed, could you get on with your life anyway? Really take a look here.

At the end of this exercise, you should now be armed with resources and ideas from earlier successful actions that you may have overlooked that you can now apply to the subject of romance. And you should start to feel a bit less worried about failure and more hopeful about your prospects for the future. At this point, anything that will enable you to feel more in control of your life will help. And the more you can identify and confront specific concerns, the more in control you're likely to be.

This is a publicity photo of my very handsome and dashing father taken in the 1940s. Despite being handsome, charming and funny—which he was until the day he died at 96—he measured his success largely in material terms. Only on rare occasions did he express doubts about his more profound success as an individual. He never fully grasped the failure of his relationship with Mother, whom he married and divorced twice. Despite the fact that they were not a good match, he never stopped loving her. I am grateful for the time I was able to spend with him at the end; it meant a great deal to both of us.

LEARNING TO EMBRACE FAILURE

*A*FTER I DID MY I'M-SO-WONDERFUL-THAT-ANY-MAN-*would-have-to-be-out-of-his-mind-not-to-want-me list, and started getting things turned around in my life* generally, I realized that as a teenager (and possibly before then), I had never felt comfortable going places or doing things by myself. I didn't feel quite complete without someone else there. I actually didn't feel that I could have fun alone, only in the company of others.

A WILLINGNESS TO FAIL

When I really looked at this area of desperation versus determination, I discovered a key point: Desperation comes from an unwillingness to fail, to lose, sometimes to extreme points of fear. It is said that animals can smell fear. Well, I believe that people can smell it, too. You just know when someone desperate is around; they make you feel uncomfortable, sometimes to a point of not wanting to be around them at all. They can actually drive you away, push you back.

To not be desperate, one must be willing to win or lose. When I looked over the popular kids in school, clearly they were not desperate. They were not afraid of being unpopular. By whatever means, whatever stroke of fate, they were confident. And you could smell that confidence on them, just as you could smell fear on someone else.

For me—and for whatever reasons—I was afraid of failure and the more I worried about being popular and having dates, the worse my fear of failure became, all leading to a quiet desperation that you could cut with a knife. So attractive!

Though I did not consider myself a noticeably desperate person at this stage of my later journey, there was still a lingering sense of fear that I couldn't be happy without a man in my life, and a concern that I would fail again. So for me, the plan to turn desperation into determination—at least to get rid of the desperate part—was going to have to include increasing my willingness to be alone comfortably, even happily (though this latter statement seemed highly unlikely at the time).

ALONE BUT NOT LONELY

I was going to have to KNOW in my heart—and experience—the joy of solitude and self-creation. It may be unreal for some of you reading this, but at that time this represented quite a challenge, but one which I knew I was going to have to conquer in order to prove to myself that I could lead a happy life, even without a man in it.

There was another reason why the ability to be comfortable by and with myself was important. In earlier relationships, I would too easily abandon my own viewpoint or ethical perspective when faced with an opposing viewpoint. I would just as likely say I agreed with someone if I believed that having a different opinion would cost me that relationship. This was not only personally damaging, but would invariably undermine the relationship I sought to save. (Who really wants to be with someone who gives in all the time to the wishes of others? Yuck!)

I'LL PICK [ME] UP AT 8!

It was the holiday season 1986. There was a movie I really wanted to see. I was dating a bit, but I couldn't think of anyone to go with on short notice, and I really wanted to see the movie. So despite the fact that it was playing downtown—quite a distance from where I lived—I decided to go solo.

I didn't feel altogether comfortable, but I had made a decision and now needed to follow through. I must tell you that while it was not my happiest "date," it was an important milestone for me. I enjoyed the movie and was glad I had gone, if alone. This was quite a victory for me. I absolutely knew that I could do it. I could do something by myself, and it was okay.

From this brief but important experience, I began to consider the possibility of never getting married again, and yet still having a rich life—not one of desperation. Because of this seemingly small victory, I felt more confident, and with that increase in confidence, I had a greater desire to discover more things that I liked and could do with or without others. The experiment was working!

Though my personal program was not over, by lessening and removing any feelings of desperation, I could begin to identify what I wanted in my life and, with determination, start to make my dreams reality.

As I have looked back on this singular experience since I began to write this book, it has become even clearer to me just how significant this change in viewpoint was and what a difference it made in my progress from this point forward. I was watching a favorite television show recently: a singing talent show. One of the celebrities on the show told a contestant that she wanted to see singers taking risks, without which they would never realize their full potential. For the opportunity to win, one must be willing to lose it all in the attempt.

This is not an invitation to stupidity, carelessness, irrational or outrageous actions! It is simply the adventure of changing one's viewpoint. Going to the movies alone was me daring my unconscious fears to do their worst, trusting that I would not die, or suffer untold embarrassment should anyone I know see me. It was a personal victory and one that changed the game for me. Living life fully is not for the faint of heart.

Chapter Five Exercises

The idea of facing one's fears is not new. Whether it's walking on hot coals, climbing the face of El Capitan in Yosemite, traversing the canopies of South American jungles—or going to the movies alone—people have experienced renewed confidence by challenging themselves.

While not as inherently dangerous, the gains from conquering one's personal fears can be just as profound and sometimes dramatic. The purpose of this exercise is to help you overcome some worry or fear you have about being alone or that in some way contributes to a feeling of desperation.

1a. For example, if you just cannot imagine spending an evening alone without watching television or listening to the news or chatting with friends, plan an evening of doing exactly that: being alone, with no TV, radio, phone calls, etc. Whatever is the fear, do exactly that (nothing dangerous here, folks, please). Only pay close attention to exactly what happens—possibly even write it down in a journal.

- What was the worst part about it?
- Did anything good happen?
- Did you faint dead away and die?
- How long were you able to resist turning on the TV, the radio, or phone friends?
- Was it longer than at other times?

If you were able to do what you most feared doing—even for a short time—give yourself a "high-5!" You did it! You may have felt uncomfortable, but you made the effort. And you didn't die over it.

1b. Then, do the exercise again and see if you can do it for a longer period of time. Build on your wins, even in small steps; you're going in the right direction and that's what's important.

The result we're going for with this exercise is **improved confidence and less desperation.** You can do it as many times as you like as long as you are heading in that direction. Then move on to the next chapter. (Remember, you can always go back and do these exercises again if you feel the need and it helps.)

Simon and Amy are my stepkids. They are great people and very much individuals which becomes obvious when they get together, especially when they get silly! They complement each other and have had each other's backs and best interests in mind since the beginning. Amy is a professional living and working in Austin, TX while Simon, who's been in the Air Force for 12 years, has just presented us with our fourth grandchild! He and Alisha have named him Jax. We heartily approve!

1 + 1 = 17 (HUH?)

*F*ROM MY EARLIER RESEARCH, I HAD COME TO REALIZE *that the happiest and brightest couples I had observed, directly or indirectly, consisted of two confident individuals who were pursuing their passions, not as rivals,* but in support of one another. Together they seemed to accomplish more of their individual as well as collective goals, and this mutual support concept was rapidly becoming part of what I envisioned for myself.

It certainly resolved the issue of giving up my personal integrity to save a relationship. The happy couples I had observed strengthened their relationships by being more and the best of themselves, not by shrinking or becoming less. Together, they were more than 1+1=2. Their power and strength grew exponentially, more like 1+1=17!

YOU ARE GREAT!

I cannot emphasize enough the importance of self-discovery and enlightenment. Not only do these things prove to the individual his or her own greatness—for we are too often reminded only of our weaknesses—but it enables the individual to be confident and not desperate for approval or attention from possible mates. And I find that when matters of the heart are rife with concerns for approval from partners, it is the road to nowhere.

People on the whole are a lot better, smarter, and nicer than they think they are. Way too much attention is given to one's failures. Not enough attention—by self and others—is given to what the individual does that is right. Too many people have a low opinion of themselves and truly, it doesn't improve their chances for success in the personal relationship business.

No matter what one's philosophical or religious preferences, anything that raises individual awareness, communication, understanding, abilities, responsibility, and joy of living, contributes to one's ability to create a lasting and loving relationship.

CHAPTER SIX EXERCISES

1a. Do something today that makes you feel smarter, happier, more intelligent, enlightened, and/or proud of yourself.

- Read something that validates your goodness, your greatness, and that directs your attention to what you've accomplished or will accomplish.
- Participate in something artful and let the aesthetics envelop you.
- Become inspired.
- If you want to feel really terrific, do something kind for someone else. Call up a friend, just 'cuz, to say hello and tell that person you were thinking of him or her.

2a. Think of a time you felt really good about yourself.

- What were you doing to bring about that feeling? If it's something you can do again, do it!

3a. Find some activity that makes you feel good and do it—just for yourself! You are much more likely to find love when you are doing those things that give you pleasure personally.

The end result of this exercise is a general feeling of being happier with yourself and a heightened sense of pride in who you are and the life you are creating.

Charley aboard our wonderful horse, Miata, at our ranch. Having horses was always part of my life's vision statement! Although it never seemed within reach and even unreal, I nonetheless longed for horses in my life. It was not until Charley and I got married that I was finally able to fulfill this forever dream of mine. He made it okay for me to enjoy my passion. He wanted me to be happy and helped make the dream come true. In spite of the fact that he is not a devoted horseperson, he has made it possible for me to have horses pretty much since we got married. This is what couples do for each other, isn't it? Help make dreams come true?

CHAPTER SEVEN

DREAM ON

FTER MY SOJOURN TO THE MOVIES WITHOUT ESCORT, *and having gotten rid of (or made adjustment to) the mental stumbling blocks that were preventing me* from being happy, I felt I was ready to take pen in hand and create my vision for the future.

THE WRONG WAY

Prior to my second marriage, I had created a Vision Statement. But because I had not discovered the real reasons for the failure of my first marriage, my Statement was more a knee-jerk reaction to that earlier marriage and, therefore, incomplete in the extreme. For example, my first husband loved me more than I loved him. So my new Statement included the idea that I would love my new husband more than I loved my first husband. There was no mention whatever of how my new honey would feel about me, so my Statement was lopsided!

When I came across the highly incomplete and inadequate Statement after my second marriage ended, I was horrified to find that I had gotten exactly what I had asked for—not what I needed or necessarily wanted, but what I <u>asked</u> for. I was determined not to make the same mistake twice! I would wait until I felt freer, calmer, saner, and more responsible before programming my fate again.

THE RIGHT WAY

Ultimately, my newest Vision Statement went on in great detail for three type-written pages (single spaced, no less). I didn't want to leave anything out; I could edit the Statement later, but for now, everything I could think of went into it. And, unlike the earlier disastrous VS, it included not only my feelings for my wished-for love, but his feelings toward me.

This time the Vision Statement included how we would treat each other, important characteristics such as humor and honesty, goals, lifestyle, sex, how we would resolve problems, physical looks, love of animals, and what life would be like.

Part of what was important to me—and was now possible because I had included everything I wanted—was that we should be in agreement on major issues, but that it wasn't so important if we didn't fully agree on smaller issues; some things were more critical than others. So one of the things I put in my Statement was that we would agree on what those important issues were.

After I wrote down everything I felt was important, I reviewed my Statement carefully to make sure that I had not left out some critical part, or that I had put something in there that I hadn't thought through enough which might trip me up later.

NO TIME TO WASTE!

Given that I had been unsuccessfully married two times already—and the fact that I was in my mid-forties—one of the elements that was important to me, and that I included in what I wrote, was that I wanted the whole process to move rather quickly. I did not want to drag out the dating thing any longer than necessary, and frankly didn't see why I should have to.

So at the very end of my Vision Statement, I did something quite risky: *I put a date on it!* A date by which I would either have met the man of my dreams, or, if he was someone I already knew, realize he was the man I had been searching for. The reason I say "risky" is because even if I didn't show the date to anyone else, it still would have been a personal loss or failure for me if I didn't pull it off. That was the risk of putting a date there—the risk of failure.

I finished my Vision Statement in late November/ early December 1986. The anticipated date of discovery: January 31, 1987.

CHAPTER SEVEN EXERCISES

1a. Draft a document describing what you want in your ideal relationship—your Vision Statement. Things to cover should include:

- Important issues for agreement and compatibility—politics, religion—anything that could potentially cause a rift if not agreed upon
- Lifestyle and finances
- How you would resolve problems
- The most important characteristics you want this mate to have
- Attitude toward kids
- Sex
- What "hats" within the relationship you'd like to wear and which ones you'd like a mate to wear
- Habits
- How you'd like to be treated and how you would treat the other person
- What kind of standards, ethics you expect
- What areas you'd like support for, such as a career or cause and how you would contribute to that person's goals

Write this as a clear picture of what your life and relationship would be like. For example: He loves me as much as I love him. We respect each other. He does/doesn't want more kids. She wants to get married, not just hang out.

Basically, you're painting a picture of the future.

Doing this document allows you to examine areas that you may not have considered before.

Be sure to cover both of your actions. If you write, "This person loves me tons," you'd better include a statement of your feelings for him or her because this thing can get pretty literal.

1b. Review your write-up. Make sure you've covered all the important points. Remember, these are YOUR important points. You're looking for someone who fulfills YOUR vision for a happy life. That's what makes it special and unique. If it's anyone else's vision—or what you think it should be based on someone else's idea of the perfect relationship and life—then it's a lie and it won't work. It only works because it represents you, and the best of you at that.

To the degree your Vision Statement promotes a better life for you and your mate—one that does not involve compromise to your personal integrity on your major issues—it will greatly contribute to the successful and happy relationship you seek.

While you can always add or modify your Statement, you may consider this exercise complete when you feel it accurately reflects what you're looking for and contains the most important points as described above.

Dad loved seeing Pearl and Lorelei when we'd visit him in Palm Springs. Fortunately, Josh and his ex-wife Liz have agreed on many areas of how to raise the girls. Pearl and Lorelei understand the concepts of being contributing members of their families; they have chores, jobs. While Lorelei loves creating music (a good job), Pearl loves to sweep! We're not sure where she comes by this talent, but one of the first things she asks when she comes to visit is "Where's the broom?!"

JOB INTERVIEW

I HAD DINNER ONE NIGHT WITH A VERY *dear and old friend who was very successful in business. I told him about my self-created program, and he* made a very good suggestion. Since people can get very serious and significant about "relationships" and everything associated with them, he suggested that I consider the subject of dating in the context of trying to fill a job.

"You have a position that's available for the right person. And you're meeting with prospective applicants to separate out the potential new-hires from the rest."

I'm not sure why that helped, but it did. I felt more relaxed and less concerned about rejection. I felt more in control, more in the driver's seat. After all, I was the one doing the interviewing and hiring!

And I felt more at ease with the prospect of dating again. Hiring someone for a job didn't have all the drama associated with it that looking for love did. *Hey, if this guy doesn't work out, I'll keep interviewing applicants until I find the right person for the job!*

It's not that I talked or acted differently on dates; I didn't suddenly become serious or businesslike. But it did make me feel more comfortable in my own mind when approaching each new dating experience. It contributed to my confidence. What was important was finding the right man for the job! (Thanks, Bill!)

CHAPTER EIGHT EXERCISES

1a. Choose an area of life that contains parallels. This area should be one:

- with which you are familiar
- that is enjoyable for you
- that doesn't have negative emotions associated with it (if you're terrified of sales, don't pick sales for your parallels)
- about which you feel comfortable

1b. Find your parallels and apply them to the dating game (you can also use the job application scenario if you like).

You may consider this exercise done when you feel more relaxed and less worried or anxious about the process of dating. The whole point is to make the process of discovery more fun, enjoyable, and less scary!

A casual Charley at our ranch. I thought he was beautiful when we met—those amazing hazel eyes and great smile—but I believe he's become more handsome over the years. A great relationship should do that for an individual. More people should expect to be happier, healthier, smarter, more productive, more attractive and having more fun as a result of their relationships. Most people have lowered their standards to such an extent— presumably so they won't be disappointed—that they've forgotten how great life can be. I'm hoping I can change their minds.

SAY WHAT?!

I REALLY WANTED WHAT WAS IN MY VISION *Statement, and believed it was worth having. Being willing to work toward finding the right person, was a very freeing notion that allowed me to* communicate more honestly and openly with men that I started dating and getting to know—not in an overpowering or aggressive manner, but freely, comfortably, and without fear of rejection (*determination* versus *desperation*).

Part of my Statement included the requirement that this man would immediately see me as the woman of his dreams, as readily as I would recognize him as the man of mine. No more of this one-sided, unrequited love thing. Been there, done that. Not fun.

A NEW KIND OF DATING EXPERIENCE

I started dating again, not many guys but, as the movie title suggests, a few good men. Each one possessed—as far as I could tell—some of the attributes that I was looking for. We would talk so I could see if it was likely to go further. There were a couple of fellows of whom I was particularly fond. In the course of conversations with each I alluded to the fact that I was attracted and wanted to get to know them better.

I was definitely not "in your face" about it. While I did want to find out sooner than later if this relationship was going anywhere, I also didn't want to make my date feel awkward or uncomfortable. Each of these fellows was someone that I wanted to keep as a friend and not scare away if it didn't work out romantically.

I think a major reason why I felt confident was because I truly wasn't worried about the outcome. And I think it was this lack of concern on my part that manifested and came through in what I was saying and how I was saying it. Words are one thing; ultimately it's your demeanor, your intention that really comes through.

At first, when I would advance the idea of moving forward in a relationship, the response was, "I like you but not in that way." Though mildly disappointed for a moment, the sting of rejection had no lasting effect. These men had not fulfilled one of my important criteria: They did not see in me what I was beginning to see in them.

DOUBTS CREEP IN

But as I continued to make new friends and get to know old friends better, two unexpected considerations began to emerge:

First, I began to lose confidence about ever really finding someone to have the qualities I had written in my Vision Statement. Perhaps I was asking for too much. Perhaps I was being unrealistic. Perhaps no one man could fit the bill.

And second, I was beginning to feel a void, an emptiness—possibly the absence of this person in my life. What I was feeling was not comfortable. In fact it was disconcerting and troublesome, but what to do about it was another matter. I just knew I had to resolve my growing doubts.

To resolve my first concern, I reviewed my Vision Statement to see if it was significantly flawed, unrealistic. Ultimately I decided that it was a good one and that the future I had painted for myself was worth pursuing. *Press on*, I told myself.

ANYONE OUT THERE?

However, I was still haunted by the notion that the person I hoped for might not actually exist. I wasn't on some ego trip—*I'm just too special for any mere mortal out there.* But I was beginning to lose hope that the person I had envisioned just didn't exist. Perhaps he would always remain an illusion.

Since I was taking a more pro-active role in my own future, I looked back at the lessons I had learned thus far in my journey to see if there was anything I had missed along the way. Then I realized that if I went into agreement that I couldn't pull it off, I was, in fact, guaranteeing my failure.

I certainly couldn't imagine a football coach in the locker room during half-time telling his team, "Well, I dunno guys if we can win this one. I know we started out really strong, but I'm beginning to think I was wrong!" One thing is certain: if you give up, you lose for sure (hardly a new concept, but one of which I needed to be reminded).

JUST NOT LOGICAL

My thought process to resolve this concern went something like this:

Okay, I exist; I am sure of my own existence. I exist on a physical as well as a spiritual plane—the "me" with all those abilities, talents, experiences, and expressions of individuality. For me to consider that there is no one out there with whom I could have a happy and satisfying relationship is to admit to an ego of unusual size and proportion! It is just not logical to suppose there is no man out there remotely as "special" as I am!

It just wasn't logical to suppose that there was no one else in the whole world like me, with similar likes, desires, goals, skills, talents, etc. (I wasn't looking for a clone of myself, but someone compatible, a good match.) I could not argue with the logic of it; in fact, it seemed really <u>illogical</u> to think otherwise.

•

CELEBRITIES

This can be a real problem for people in the public eye. By virtue of their unique positions, they are already in a minority group. It would be easy for such people to conclude that there just isn't enough good mate-material out there. When those thoughts become self-created future realities, the losses can mount up. If such individuals feel this way, their options are (a) to compromise with their standards, and/or (b) continue to make the same mistakes to prove how right were their original "conclusions." ("You see, men CAN'T be trusted!" "Women are only after me for my money.") Either way, it's a no-win situation.

There was a time when I had come to the conclusion that (a) all the good men were already taken, and (b) there weren't enough available men in the crowd I hung out with. In retrospect, I truly believe that if a great guy had walked up and kissed me, I wouldn't have seen him because I couldn't "see" what I believed wasn't there to begin with!

•

LOGIC AND FAITH

Faced with the truth of the sheer volume of people on this planet—many of them men—and the growing reality that surely there was one out there as a suitable mate, I was ready to face another obvious reality: This person already existed! I might not know where he was or what he looked like, but the fact that he wasn't in my life at the time, didn't mean he didn't exist. He was somewhere doing something! And that got me to wondering, *Where is he now? What's he doing now?*

And then things started getting interesting! I made some sort of *connection* with this "someone." What's more, I felt I <u>knew</u> this person deeply, the sort of person he was. He was real to me. Although it must have seemed like a leap of faith, I <u>knew</u> that he existed, that he had a life right now. The more I believed in this reality, the more excited I got at the prospect of wondering what his life was like while I pursued mine. The void I had felt was gone! I did not feel empty anymore. In fact I felt happy and confident I was still in the game and closer to my goals.

(**Note:** For as long as I can remember—including recollections as an infant—I've known that I was a spiritual being and that people are first and foremost spiritual entities, not bodies, as the materialists would have us believe. All the creativity, compassion, love, goodness, integrity, and courage spring from the spirit; there is not a piece of meat anywhere, including the brain—a wonderful switchboard for the body—that is the source of individual expression and creativity.)

Chapter Nine Exercises

1a. If you are currently seeing anyone or more than one person, how does that person begin to align or not align with your "job description?" Do you need to spend more time with that person to find out enough to know how he or she stacks up? If so, find a way to spend more time, but be sure to engage in enough communication to discover what that person's thoughts and realities are, generally and concerning you.

(If that's all you did during those get-togethers, you will have accomplished a lot! Remember this is a discovery process. Don't fail to give that person insight on your realities, too.

1b. Do this with each person you're seeing socially. This is pretty much an ongoing drill, so don't think you're going to be "done" with it in a day or two; it takes as long as it takes, so be patient. However, if you find that right person quickly, don't think you have to continue seeing other people either! It's not about time. It's about <u>discovery.</u> Once you find your prize, acknowledge it!

2a. On the matter of communicating comfortably and freely with prospective mates: Before you get too deeply into expressing your feelings for someone, first consider what *effect* you hope to create by communicating.

- Do you want to retain the person as a friend if that's all he or she wants it to be?
- Do you want that person to feel comfortable and safe in communicating his or her feelings toward you?
- How could you communicate in order to accomplish the effect you're going for?

If you are mindful of creating a safe environment in which the other person can communicate honestly and freely, you will be listening and really understanding that person's viewpoint, which you should really acknowledge. Too many times, people are made to feel wrong for speaking up, for being honest. So people become shy about their feelings and/or say things they hope will be at least socially acceptable or politically-correct if not heartfelt.

You don't have to go there. When you are confident in yourself, and not desperate and worried about failure, you are more likely to create a safe environment in which real and meaningful communication can occur.

2b. Practice this concept of defining the effect you want to create and going about creating it. Try it with friends, perhaps on subjects that are touchy or uncomfortable to discuss. It's like magic! When you feel confident that you can do this, try it with people you're dating. It's not about being pushy. It's about a lovely and gentle honesty that acknowledges and respects people's different viewpoints, without losing one's own viewpoint.

3a. If you doubt that someone special for you already exists, really take a look at the reality of it. It's not necessary to *make a connection* in order to wonder what this person is doing now. Or to wonder what he or she looks like and if it's someone you already have met...or not. I found it fun to wonder how I would meet this person—notice I said "how" not "if."

At this point, the confidence you have in being able to reach your goal should be increasing sufficiently that you "believe" there is someone out there, possibly (and hopefully) looking for you, too! If not, go back and redo earlier exercises that address confidence.

Granddaughter Diana—13 going on 30! I love this photo that Charley took several years ago. (She has a way with the camera, not unlike my mother, her grandmother.) At almost 20, she has shown herself to be a talented artist, writer and photographer. And though she provided us with some not-uncommon teenage drama, she's proven herself to be bright, intelligent, sweet and a very strong young lady who's gotten back to her own life's vision statement. How nice to contribute an ethical and productive family member into society.

THROWING OUT THE BABY OR THE BATH WATER?

*W*ITH RENEWED CONFIDENCE, I CONTINUED TO *use the Vision criteria to evaluate the men I was seeing, but soon found myself struggling again. This time,* the source of my problem was part of an old game I had played—another negative game, not one at which I could win. I had created this sort of document before. Let's say it contained ten different qualities or attributes that I wanted. But then I'd meet some guy that fulfilled maybe two or three of the noted attributes, fall madly in love, decide that *he was it*, and immediately abandon the list!

(Do you remember the scene in the movie "Cinderella" how the Prince's representative tried to fit Cinderella's glass slipper onto the oversized feet of the stepsisters? Well, it just didn't fit, no matter how they tried cramming their size 12 feet into that size 5 slipper. And *wishing* the shoe would fit didn't make it happen either.)

PRIORITIES

In the past, when I'd think I'd found "Mr. Right" prematurely, I'd toss the list and pursue the guy, ultimately unsuccessfully. I'd spend my time trying to figure out how to cram my Vision Statement into the guy, instead of making sure the guy fit the VS. So on the two occasions that came up in my recent dating experiences—when my priorities shifted to The Guy—I rededicated myself to making the Statement the priority. The man would have to fit my requirements and the life that it meant, or he wasn't The Guy.

Keep in mind that I had really gotten to a point where I was confident in the future I had envisioned—confident that I could have it, confident that it was worth pursuing. And I had reviewed the Statement to make sure that it reflected what I really wanted. Since one of my criteria was a mutual recognition by each other of each other as love interests, to go off pursuing some fellow who did not see me that way, would have been really counter-productive.

Those of you reading this may not have that as a requirement, and that's just fine, because you have to work out your priorities as I had to work out mine. It's just that for me, I did not want to prolong the beginning of the rest of my life. I still had a lot of living to do and was ready to start!

BACK TO THE TRUTH

Ultimately, I had to make a decision. If the Vision I proclaimed truly and honestly reflected my goals, abandoning its ideals would lead me away from the future I was trying to create. If I abandoned my personal integrity on this one, the relationship was doomed to failure! *Don't do it!* was my admonition. If I felt that strongly about someone, I could always re-examine my Vision Statement and change it. But there had better be some really compelling reasons.

By this time I had enough confidence to recognize that anxiety over someone—*I just have to have him in my life!*—was a red flag. What I really needed to do in that situation was to find someplace quiet and get my head on straight. In the final analysis, the man was going to have to fit into my Vision Statement, or he wasn't the right man.

Chapter Ten Exercises

1a. If you find yourself abandoning the criteria to pursue someone who does not fulfill at least the really important, big priorities, review your Vision Statement and either re-dedicate yourself to finding Mr. or Ms. Right per the criteria, or change the Statement to better reflect your new priorities.

1b. If you doubt that your VS is a clear picture of what you want, inspect it until you are certain and re-examine the person you're pursuing in light of the modifications you've since made.

(Note: If you feel overwhelmed with sexual passion, you'd better really look at how long that relationship will last in the absence of all the other things in life that command attention and come up over time. Physical attraction is part of having a great relationship—it's part of what makes this type of relationship different from others. But it won't hold up over time if that's all there is to it, period. If you don't believe that, look at some of the very sexy movie stars that get married then wind up in divorce court because their very sexy spouses cheated on them!)

The wedding day: February 28, 1987. Charley, Dad and I in front. Brother, Mark, and son, Josh, behind. We had a big western bash with bales of hay, horses, a western band, line dancing, music, a barbeque and a preacher who dressed all in black and who carried a shotgun! It was amusing to see how people reacted when Charley showed up to our wedding in my Cadillac with his ex-wife Mary Kay (I had to take his truck to bring the very large cake earlier in the day). Such a fun wedding!

THE BIG FURNITURE CAPER

*I*T WAS THE CHRISTMAS SEASON *1986. I WAS very busy going to parties and generally enjoying myself. All during this* time, I continued to meet with friends and continued to communicate with "prospective applicants."

In January I had decided to take some furniture to a friend's estate sale about 20 miles away. My friend had loaned me his truck, but I needed someone to help load the items from my garage into the truck as I couldn't lift them unassisted. I lived in a lovely community in Southern California called Toluca Lake, one block from my friend Peter Green's art and graphics studio. In fact, I was doing business with Peter on behalf of the company for which I was then working. It was great. I could go over late at night and Peter was sure to be there working on some movie poster or the like.

I knew two men who would likely help me load the furniture onto the truck, assuming they were around when I needed help. I couldn't get a hold of one of them, but Charley worked for Peter, and though we had only recently been introduced (actually, he was so unassuming that I didn't know what he did exactly), I knew he was nice and would probably help, which he agreed to do.

TAKE CARE OF ME?

Charley showed up Saturday morning; I was still in bed (bad form). After keeping him waiting a short while, I accompanied him to the garage. Without help, he lifted a heavy chair onto the bed of the truck. Out of nowhere, I had this overwhelming sense that this person—this almost-stranger—was someone who could take care of me! The strength and random nature of that feeling shocked me.

All I needed him to do was help me load up the truck. That was all. But he asked how I was going to get the furniture off the truck when I got to my destination. I didn't know. He offered to drive with me and unload the items at the other end. I accepted his gracious offer and off we went.

Because it was my friend's truck, I did the driving. The entire trip consisted of an endless stream of chatter, punctuated only by moments of breathing. The subject matter was diverse, from movies we liked to deeply felt opinions on business and photography, living in the country, politics, philosophy, world religions and people in general.

And then, with great enthusiasm, Charley said "I love you!" *What! Men don't say things like! Girlfriends do, but men—as a general rule—don't!*

But here he was telling me he loved me! There was no lust in his voice or manner, just affection and friendship and, perhaps, recognition of mutual realities. Nonetheless, here was another unexpected and startling moment in this relationship that was only a couple of hours old!

Yes, I thought, *it must be that we share so many interests! And how refreshing that is! Yes, that's it.*

STRANGE FEELINGS

At some point on the return trip, we stopped at a fast food place. Charley asked me if I wanted something to eat; I said "No," preferring to stay in the truck. After he went in, however, I suddenly had the desire for food. Once inside the restaurant, however, I had this uncontrollable urge to run to him, throw my arms around him, and kiss him like a long-lost and dear friend who'd just been found on some remote island following a boating accident 20 years before! Inches before crashing into him, I stopped short. It must have looked peculiar to Charley and anyone close by.

What the heck is going on here?!

We drove back to my place (Charley was now driving). I invited him to dinner as a gesture of thanks for his help, but he declined saying he had to return to work. However, we did arrange to have dinner on Monday. Though I felt uncomfortable with my feelings, I also knew that he was someone very special, a man with whom I could be good friends. So when Monday came, we walked to and from the restaurant, talking all the way there and back, which was becoming the routine. It was an enjoyable evening.

CLUB DATE

A friend of mine was appearing at a trendy club in Santa Monica on Wednesday night, two days hence. I invited Charley to go with me. He drove my car, a Cadillac Seville (which was nicer than his little truck). We had a great time and on the way home, we again talked and talked, seemingly never running out of things to discuss. "Do you think you'd ever marry again?" It just seemed like another question out of many. "Yes, I would like to," I replied matter-of-factly.

"By the way," he said casually, "how old are you?" "Forty-five." He didn't bat an eye. "And you?" I replied. "Just turned twenty-nine." I was crestfallen. If there had only been a three where the two now stood—even a three "zero" would have been okay, but a two? My heart sank.

As it turned out, even at his age, he had been married twice before, and both times to women older than himself. The age difference was a bigger issue for me than it was for him, obviously. But as I became more comfortable with the subject at hand, we continued talking.

CONFESSION TIME

Once at my place, I decided I had to talk to him about the way I was feeling, even if he just wanted to be friends and nothing more. Despite the fact that we had only just met, I was drawn to him. Minimally, I knew he was the sort of person who would listen and understand, and not "freak out!"

So I blurted it out: "I have to talk to you. I think I'm falling in love with you, and I don't understand it at all. In fact, I feel very strange about the whole thing. And if you just want to be friends, well that's okay, but I just had to tell you." Then I told him about all the other feelings I had had: him lifting the chair and my thoughts, the fast-food restaurant and almost colliding into him, my concerns about the age difference—well, just everything. He listened intently, not giving a clue as to his inner-most thoughts. How would this conversation end?

HIS TURN

"Well," he said when I was done, "I fell in love with you the first time I saw you at Peter's studio a few weeks ago. And every time you came in on business, I'd go to Peter and find out everything I could about you: where you lived, if you were seeing anybody and if so, who, what your background was—just everything!"

(I was, in fact, more prepared for polite rejection than his undying affection.)

"When you asked me to help you load some furniture last Saturday, I actually had to work, but I wasn't about to pass up an opportunity to spend time with you. I just knew I had to, so I did. I wanted to stay so badly for dinner, but just couldn't, but I was so tempted!"

I sat down next to him on the couch (I had made my speech standing—perhaps to flee if necessary after my out-pouring). We kissed and kissed. Was I dreaming?

Interrupted only by work, we were inseparable. Charley didn't have a lot of money, and the prospect of starting over at 45 had not been part of my Vision Statement. But it was only an issue for 30 seconds. I didn't need to know more *about* Charley; I *knew Charley* and I knew he was the man with whom I wanted to spend the rest of my life. The man I knew before I knew him.

On Friday of that week, we talked about what the next step for us might be. We could have lived together, but it seemed to us that the only logical next step was marriage. We knew we wanted to be together for the rest of our lives. Both Charley and I liked the institution of marriage.

Neither of us felt trapped by it and liked the fact that it was a very public commitment we would be making in the company of family and friends.

THE WEDDING!

Though we tried several times to elope, it was pointless. Our respective work schedules, the schedules of our kids (really, the only ones we felt strongly should be in attendance), and the desire of our friends to throw us a big wedding, all conspired to make us wait, if only for a week or two. And so it was that exactly four Saturdays from the day of the Big Furniture Caper, Charley and I got married. It was a big western bash, complete with a western band, bales of hay, horses, a barbeque, western dancing, and a preacher who walked around in black boots, hat, and a long black coat, carrying a shotgun!

Over 100 people showed up for our quickly-thrown-together affair. And Peter, an extraordinary and well-published caricaturist, drew pictures of us for the wedding invitations. As one dear friend put it, "I just knew when I saw the two of you together, that this was a match made in Heaven!" Apparently the gods agree, because after 26 years, things are just getting better and better in every possible way!

BLISS

As much as I had a vision of what I wanted my future to be, I could not have imagined how it would unfold. One can certainly envision an outcome, dream a dream, pray or wish for something in the future. But it's more difficult, if not downright impossible, to envision all the ways or routes by which the goal will be achieved. (Remember that quote from W.H. Murray earlier in this book? You might want to read it again.)

And this is a good thing because not in a million years could I have planned the way we met. I never would have imagined or conceived that asking someone to help move some furniture would be the method of finding the love of my life. And if I had tried to micro-manage the process—and "planned" how we would meet—I wouldn't have planned the way it happened and would have missed the opportunity when it presented itself.

GROWING TOGETHER

What I do know, for sure, is that whatever led to my resolve so many years ago to have a lasting and loving relationship, also allowed me to grow as an individual. Life has challenges and conditions change, but I cannot imagine another person with whom I'd rather spend my life than my wonderful husband, Charley.

We sometimes laugh at all the "firsts" we've had as a couple, and how many of the same oddball things we'd done while leading separate lives before we met. Together we've accomplished things that we're quite certain neither of us, alone, would have even considered doing, let alone at which we could succeed.

We are each better for our relationship. Our kids are better for it, as are our friends and even our communities. And on those very rare occasions that either one of us is ill, there is nothing quite like having your best friend taking care of you.

We never tire of each other's company. We're never bored. For most of our married lives, we've also worked together—a challenge for most couples. We still laugh a lot. I can't say enough good things about him to others, while he loves bragging about me and my accomplishments and still calls me his "trophy wife." Imagine that!

There is no jealousy and never has been in our relationship. In fact, one of the traits I most admired in Charley when we first met was that he spoke well of and with admiration for his ex-wife—a very rare thing. It was a glimpse into his soul and I loved him for it.

We've continued to grow as individuals; I believe that is important. But all the traits and characteristics that I had wanted so long ago in a life partner were the things that defined Charley and still do: the core virtues such as personal integrity, romance, consideration, affection, intellect (and did I mention great buns?!).

CHAPTER ELEVEN EXERCISES

This one you're going to have to create yourself! This is, after all, <u>your</u> story and <u>your</u> life. I am excited for you and the future you are creating! Actually, there is an exercise here: Your final exam!

1. When you've accomplished what you hoped for, write and let me know about it so I can share in your wins. That is why I wrote this book after all— that others might have rich and wonderful lives full of joy and laughter and accomplishment and love.

Thank you for doing your part!

This was our holiday card a year after we got married. (Even with a few extra pounds, Charley found me attractive.) I must say that despite the failures that I had experienced in the past, I was deliriously happy being married, but only because it was to the right person. I wish nothing more than for others to experience this same level of happiness, especially since it doesn't require that one give up who one is in the process. If one has to be someone or something else to satisfy a relationship, there's something wrong.

REFLECTIONS–
LESSONS LEARNED
AND RELEARNED

*I*N THE INTERVENING YEARS SINCE CHARLEY *and I got married, I've had a chance to reflect on my life and* how being happily married has changed it so dramatically.

Many years ago, Charley told me that he felt that making a relationship "official" by getting married was important. He felt that making a very public statement about a commitment you were making, somehow put the future there for that relationship that just living together didn't.

Further, that in making that public commitment, you were asking your friends and family to not only witness and support that commitment, but to contribute to its creation into the future even if at times that meant stepping in to help when things weren't going well. (Little did our friends and family know what they were getting themselves into when they accepted our wedding invitation!)

It all sounds rather daunting at first glance, but being married has been the most joyful and fun experience Charley or I could have imagined. Formalizing our love and commitment through the instrument we call marriage was just the right thing to do.

A GROWING TREND

There seems to be a growing trend among young people today to just live together rather than get married. If this is the case, I can hardly blame them for being wary of the institution, especially with media's preoccupation with celebrity bad marriages, divorce, cheating antics, sexual misbehavior—whether such stories are exaggerated or not.

Such widely-publicized exploits—viewed day in and day out—tend to become the new and pervasive reality. But is it reality? Real or not, such images surrounding us can make even die-hard optimists start to believe that life just isn't that fun anymore, the solution being to settle for less to avoid disappointment.

A YOUTHFUL PERSPECTIVE

It was therefore an unexpected pleasure to hear from the recently-married son of dear friends. He had known his bride for nine years; they had pretty much grown up together. Shortly after he returned from their honeymoon, he told me that he was very glad they had gotten married; that somehow it was different, better, than just living together. He couldn't say for sure why but he did feel there was a difference and one which he had not expected. It felt good!

MORE GOOD NEWS!

In promoting my book, I've come to meet some lovely people in radio and television, print media and public relations. In telling my story, many of those people have shared their stories with me—stories of their happy and loving marriages. They had found their soul-mates and been in these fulfilling relationships for many years.

Suddenly I found myself surrounded by happy and happily-married individuals—all of them happy to have someone with whom to share their personal journeys! The more I talked with these folks, the more I saw consistencies from my story to theirs. It was validating that the lessons I had learned were universal—that they were relevant to men and women alike, and to people of all ages and experiences.

It was also especially exciting to me that the actual reality is that there are many happy people out there that we never hear about, whose lives go on without fanfare, yet who enjoy lives of love and pleasure, commitment, shared challenges, rewards and accomplishments.

For me, this may be the biggest thrill of this whole experience of sharing my story—that there are other, similar stories out there—stories that need to be told to help create a new and better reality as an inspiration to others.

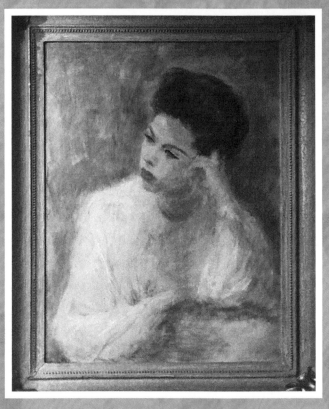

This oil painting was done of Mother in 1942 when she was pregnant with me. It was painted by my aunt, Helen Omansky Gross, a brilliant artist who worked in all media—oils, pastels, acrylics, watercolor, bronze, colored glass, clay, alabaster, marble. This painting hangs over the mantelpiece in our dining room. Mother looks as reflective and sad as I know she was—a personal tragedy on many levels because she was such an inspiration to me.

REFLECTIONS—
PERSONAL INTEGRITY

*L*IKE THE WORD "RESPONSIBILITY," *the words "personal integrity" may instantly conjure up remembrances of failures,* inadequacies, moments of being less than honorable. So let me first clarify what I mean and what I'm talking about here.

For one thing, not one of us is free of sin at some time or other. None of us. True, some folks (maybe even you) have been a bit too "creative" when it came to being untruthful or even unfaithful. Instead let's take our attention off of the past long enough for me to share my thoughts with you as to why I believe having some personal integrity is <u>vital</u> to your quest for love.

What I mean by *personal integrity* is doing one's level best to be decent and honest; keeping one's agreements (assuming such agreements are constructive rather than destructive); trying one's hardest to face difficult situations with an eye toward solving problems and not just complaining; and trying a bit harder to do what's right despite temptations to run away.

It is certainly not about perfection, but making the effort to improve one's own conduct and to help others in the process. It may also include making up for prior transgressions.

CRIMINALS AND LOVERS

It is not a new concept that criminals leave clues behind their crime scenes so that they'll get themselves caught. Perfect crimes, if there are such things, are committed by people whose basic goodness is so deeply buried, they don't allow themselves the luxury of attempted self-correction. We generally call these people anti-social or sociopaths. But for your garden-variety criminal, he or she leaves clues.

Why?

No matter how arrived at, most people (again, except the thoroughly and ruthlessly depraved) know right from wrong and recognize that inner voice when they hear it. Whether this concept is arrived at through religious conviction and belief, or through an innate certainty, people know when they've done something that violates their moral or ethical codes.

When Johnny steals cookies from the cookie jar after Mama told him not to, he knows he "done wrong" when he takes the cookies, no matter how he then justifies his actions—if only to himself.

Knowing what was right to begin with, Johnny "self-corrects" by leaving crumbs on the corners of his mouth or gets sick or gets cookies stolen from him at school ... or, or, or.

When a love partner breaks faith with his or her significant other, he or she will find a way to self-punish—maybe not in the current relationship, but almost surely in a subsequent relationship. I've seen it happen too many times—sometimes up close and personal—to believe anything differently.

A husband cheats on his wife. To throw others off the scent of his transgression, he complains about her, pinpointing her faults, her failures. He leaves her for another, leaving devastation in his wake.

She eventually recovers and moves on. He cheats on his new wife with another. They divorce, leaving children to cope. He becomes sick, has problems at work, financial difficulties.

Self-punishment.

SNAKES OF ONE KIND OR ANOTHER

I'm not suggesting that we feel sorry for such a person. Truth be told, it is his basic concept of right and wrong that's at the core of why he brings about his own self-destruction. When you understand the concept, you don't have to hate the person. But it does mean that you have to be mindful of not becoming part of the self-destruct either.

When we lived at our ranch we had to contend with rattlesnakes. They were a fact of daily life. I studied some about their behavior and never hated or even disliked them. But I sure as hell wasn't going to let them near my grandchildren or animals. If I couldn't figure out a humane way to get rid of them (take them far away from my property), or if they insisted on coming back, off with their heads.

The point is that to the degree people know, in their hearts, right from wrong, and act in a manner they know to be destructive to others, they will have issues and problems that prevent them from experiencing the happiness they ultimately would like to experience.

Have you ever wondered why when you, the recipient of such transgressions, tried to be kind and understanding to someone like our human "snake" above, he or she became more upset with you? Perhaps you interrupted that person's self-punishment. You don't have to be unkind, but it helps if you understand what you may be looking at.

Only by recognizing their own responsibility for their actions—and by making attempts to redeem themselves—will they begin to allow themselves some happiness.

I know this from personal experience. At the end of my second marriage, I had to distance myself from my then stepson, whom I adored. To do otherwise would have been very selfish of me, and would have compromised his relationship with his father, whom he also loved.

Ultimately, my stepson and I were reunited and are friends to this day. I knew what I did was the ethically correct thing to do for his sake at that time. I know that acting on what I knew to be right, despite the personal sacrifice it meant, allowed me to have a clear conscience that contributed to my finding true and abundant love.

The take-away from this section: If need be, clean up your act and keep it clean or life will find a way to clean it for you!

My brother, Mark, and his wife, Barbara, have been an inspiration to me for many years. They are a great couple and great people. Together, they have had many adventures and have helped each other fulfill individual and collective goals. Mark and I are close and I can't imagine having a better person as my brother. Like Simon and Amy, Mark and I usually get a good case of the 'sillies' when we get together, sometimes laughing so vigorously it's hard to breath! I so love those moments!

CHAPTER FOURTEEN

REFLECTIONS– GOOD PEOPLE = GREAT COUPLES!

GREAT COUPLES, GREAT MATCHES, *are made up of good people. I just haven't seen anything to convince me otherwise.*

Again, we're not talking about perfection here. Each of us is flawed. Each of us has strengths and weaknesses. But I have yet to see lasting relationships between loving individuals made up of anything less than two really good and decent people.

MARRIAGE: STEPPING STONE TO GREATER POSSIBILITIES!

For me, marriage should be a further jumping off point for exploring the rest of life and its many possibilities. (The first foundation should be the individual, him- or herself, from which all else becomes possible.) If you start with two good people, you have a much better chance of forming a relationship that nurtures both individuals toward individual and common goals and dreams, including those beyond the family.

I have mentioned this before, but it bears repeating: Charley and I have accomplished more as a couple—on many levels—than either had previously accomplished as single individuals.

Great relationships are not made from one dominant person and his or her subservient partner. Or out of the pairing of one smart and giving individual and an emotional parasite. Or, for that matter, two terribly weak individuals like two alcoholics who "help" each other in support of their destructive habits.

If these things I mention are even half true, there is no downside to bettering oneself and doing one's best to improve toward being the sort of individual who can create and enjoy love in his or her life.

I have written about my son Josh being an inspiration to raise my standards. Truly, during and following my last marriage, he was the gold standard by which I subsequently measured the richness of my life. Everything had to rise to the level of enjoyment, fulfillment, support and fun that was my relationship with him. Happily, I can say that I have accomplished just that in all areas of my life. Josh continues to be a best friend. My life is richer with him in it.

REFLECTIONS– ARE WE HAVING FUN YET?!

AVE YOU BY CHANCE NOTICED *that these last chapter titles have included a great deal of exclamation points?*

There's a reason for that. I love my life! And the more I live it, the more excited I get about it and the possibilities that await in my future!

RAISING STANDARDS

When I started regaining control over my life after the break-up of my last marriage, I had occasion to look at my life to see if there was anything in it—any area, any individual—about which I was perpetually excited and happy. If I could find such an area or person, I would know that this at least was an aspect of my life that I had gotten right. And at that time, I was looking for ways to have been right against an avalanche of wrongness.

I indeed found such an area in my relationship with my wonderful son, Josh! I was not married when I became pregnant. He and I were very close right from the start. I always considered him my friend. I always talked to him knowing he would understand my intentions, if not the words.

The bond that we had was rock solid. And for the most part, our relationship was free of conflict. (Although, he did tell me, in no uncertain terms, that I should not marry my last husband! He was, as it turned out, right; I shouldn't have married him. I should have listened.)

THE NEW STANDARD

From that moment, I determined to make every area of my life bring me the joy and enthusiasm as did the relationship with Josh—such areas including my physical and spiritual self, my career, my passions and hobbies, my environmental goals, and most certainly my love life.

It wasn't a goal I especially kept track of, but in 2010 I realized that I had, in fact, accomplished exactly that! There is nothing I am currently doing or in which I'm deeply involved that is not of my own choosing, that I am not passionate about, that doesn't bring me extreme joy and fulfillment, and that doesn't help others.

I am passionate about my life! I have my beloved horses with me. And in that, I found Bazan, my dream horse. My beautiful 115-pound dog Roxy is the dearest thing possible. And the two cats, Pye and Milo, are as perfect as cats can be.

My home is warm and inviting. I am surrounded by beauty and works of art. There is music in this home and many musical friends with whom to share it. And I am singing again—mostly jazz—and having so much fun!

I have what I believe to be the best friends in the world—each a gem in his or her own right. And I've reunited with old friends to share fond memories and laughter. (I selected well with these friends, too, as they are just as upbeat and awesome in the present as they were when we first met—in some cases, over fifty years ago!)

My son and stepkids, Simon and Amy, are the best! Truly, I couldn't be more proud of each and every one of them. The grandchildren are very special to me. Diana will be 20 next year and is on her way to fulfilling her dreams. Pearl and Lorelei are growing so beautifully. Each is talented and kind and loving. And a fourth grandbaby, a boy named Jax, is the newest from Simon and Alisha.

Obviously, I'm passionate about this book along with the products and services to follow in its wake, including opportunities to do more public speaking which I love to do!

Need I say that I'm also passionate about my husband and marriage? Is this not the reason for all of this excitement?!

(If all of this over-the-top enthusiasm is getting tiresome and on your nerves, I'm done....at least for now!)

Exercise: Find something about your life that you absolutely LOVE! Let that be the new standard for everything you do for the rest of your life. Don't make less of your goals and dreams. And don't listen to naysayers who tell you that you can't have what you want in life.

It is unfortunate, but some people act-out in the misguided belief that the only way for them to feel important and successful in life is by squashing and making nothing of those around them. It's not rational, but like you would treat the rattlesnakes at our ranch, don't allow yourself to get in harm's way.

If you do anything with such people, try to show them, by your example if you can, how rich life can be. If they're unwilling to put in the time and effort to improve their own lives, get on with yours!

When you select the right person to share your life, your life gets better. Here we are at our 5 ½-acre place in Utah, having fun like two kids. Our garage, behind us, was 1,500 sq. ft.—larger than the house we moved into on our return to So. California a year later. So who's acting his or her age here? Can you tell who's younger than who? Doubtful, because we were both being equally silly. And we still laugh a lot all these years later.

CHAPTER SIXTEEN

REFLECTIONS— *THE* SECRET TO LASTING RELATIONSHIPS

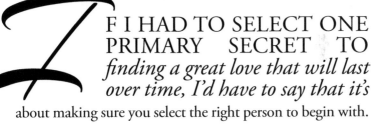 F I HAD TO SELECT ONE PRIMARY SECRET TO *finding a great love that will last over time, I'd have to say that it's* about making sure you select the right person to begin with.

There is an old adage in real estate that you make your money back on an investment in real estate when you <u>buy</u>, not when you *sell*. Good selection of a property in which to invest is the key to getting a good return on your investment over time.

The same applies to finding a soul-mate. (Come to think of it, this principle applies to *any* long-term relationship you are seeking, whether personal, professional, or political.)

Yes, you want romance. Yes, you want physical attraction. Yes, you want to feel that special something. And if you select well to begin with, you can have all of those things for a lifetime!

But you must also select someone with whom you can collaborate when times are tough and challenging—someone who can depend upon <u>you</u> in crises just as you should be able to depend upon him or her. You should also select someone with mutual overall goals and objectives so you're both going in the same direction when it comes to solving problems or making major decisions.

If this sounds dry and boring, please know that some of Charley's and my best times and adventures were slogging through awful situations. We look back on these adventures with some relish and good humor—another important asset in any relationship.

Rather than say we "work" at our relationship—which, after all, sounds somewhat painful and a lot like, well, **wooork**—we vigorously create our relationship into the future. That's a more fun way to view it. Plus, it happens to be the truth.

I did not have an easy life, but whenever I'd spend time with my animals, everything seemed brighter and more positive. Charley and I currently have five animal friends, not counting the five koi: two cats, one dog and two horses. This is Roxy, our 115-pound So. African mastiff whom we adopted when she was eight. Roxy is such a perfect match for Charley and me and our current lifestyle. It's actually been that way with all our current pets. After various false starts, we got it right on our selections. We are indeed one big happy family!

CHAPTER SEVENTEEN

REFLECTIONS—
ONE FINAL THOUGHT

*S*TOP BLAMING YOUR PARENTS, YOUR BROKEN *home, your poverty, your abusive uncle, your lack of education or opportunity, your DNA and gene-pool—* everything and anyone—for the lack of meaningful love in your life.

Notwithstanding the fact that these things can and do happen in life—and acknowledging the negative impact of such misfortunes which indeed exist as a reality—your prospects for future happiness will not measurably improve until you start owning the realities of your life in all their many colors and hues, good or bad.

Nothing great ever occurs without personal assumption of responsibility and causation. Even with an abiding belief in God, the individual must take part in the creation of his or her life.

I have not had an easy life myself. My mother was an alcoholic and pill taker. It was a not uncommon occurrence for Mother, Mark and me to escape our surroundings in the middle of the night to get away from some boyfriend or husband not always knowing where we'd end up by morning. Despite Mother making light of such "adventures," she did not provide a good example of how people should live, behave or grow up.

Mother was a dear and wonderful, kind individual. But her life was a mess—no shining examples for me to emulate or follow on multiple levels.

Life is tough, sometimes very tough. It can be unkind and unjust and unfair. I know of no one whose life has been entirely spared of conflict and drama, even when those individuals grew up in "normal" homes with a decent parent or parents. The fact that some people come from homes and situations in which they are immersed in such drama and conflict is a real tragedy.

It's just that if you want to improve your situation and have a better and more rewarding life, you can start by acknowledging that for better or worse, wittingly or unwittingly, <u>you were there</u> when it all went down— sometimes a stinging reality to embrace, but I believe an important one to attempt, even in small ways. Fortunately, the potential for rewards in the future as a result of facing one's fears and past, can make it well worth the effort!

This may seem like an odd photo to place next to the Epilogue. But if you get nothing from this candid shot other than the fact that I'm clearly happy, that will do. I am a very happy and satisfied woman. I have a great life. I started out this life with a lot of potential, but since meeting and marrying Charley, that potential has increasingly become reality. And amazingly, there seems to be no end in sight to what I am capable of doing—and will manifest—for the duration. So much of what makes life worth living is how many people you can help along the way. I guess that means that I'll be happier yet!

EPILOGUE

HORTLY AFTER CHARLEY AND I WERE MARRIED, I CAME *across my Vision Statement— which, after Charley and I got together, I had "retired" to a desk drawer since it had* done its job. On it, that risky date of discovery—January 31, 1987—a date I plucked from the air with no thought of the impossibility of my decision; the date of my resolve; and the date Charley helped me move furniture and we discovered each other.

Whether you are as fortunate as I have been, and whether or not you pick a date and it doesn't work out, do not abandon your dream. You are important. People need you and you deserve to be happy. The world needs you and your contributions, and you are more likely to make those contributions when you are happy with yourself and your life. I am so convinced that this is true, that I consider it *unethical* for you <u>not</u> to be happy!

In looking back on my mistakes, pretty much all of them could have been avoided if I had been willing to <u>look</u> at what was in front of me and had the courage to act on what I saw. It is true that the truth shall set you free.

Learn everything you can about yourself and life. Seek counsel with honest people, with friends, with family, and your spiritual leaders. Do your best and if you fail, realize that your decisions were the best ones you could come up with at the time.

And do not for a minute believe the notion that meaningful love springs from or is improved by neuroses. It does not. Love springs from what is good and right about people. A very dear friend once told me that you find true love when you are being yourself and doing those things which are true to your nature and which give you pleasure and pride.

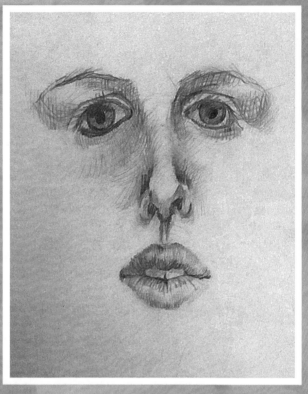

When I drew this self-portrait I was living in Washington, D.C. It was July of 1963, my first time away from home and just shy of my 21st birthday. I had no idea at the time how significant living in D.C. would be. I was there for the Martin Luther King march in August of that year and saw it up close. I was at a local tavern on that fateful day in November when word came through that President John F. Kennedy had been shot; living in D.C. somehow made it more personal for me. From the roof of the building where I worked for a national magazine, I could see the funeral procession on Connecticut Avenue where the Kennedys and world leaders converged on St. Matthew's Cathedral a block away. It was also a time of profound joy doing musical comedy with the American Light Opera Company in beautiful Georgetown with its cobblestone streets and French row houses. I had no idea then what adventures awaited me. And now that I know what all those adventures have been I can honestly say that I have no regrets. The high points will be with me always. And even the low moments gave me pause to reflect and learn. No down-sides, just personal growth. I am excited about what adventures await me for the next 50 years! Hey, anything is possible!

LIFE
ACKNOWLEDGEMENTS

I KNOW, A PAGE FOR ACKNOWLEDGEMENTS *is supposed to be at the beginning of a book. But as I was thinking about those people who helped along the* way, I realized that if you hadn't read this book—and didn't know if you were going to like it or not—why would you care about those who helped make it possible? Hmmm…

I hope that you have come away from this reading experience with something positive, and something to help you greatly improve your chances of creating love and happiness in your life.

For I believe, with all my heart, that if this old planet is going to survive and improve, it will be because people of goodwill—finding more points of agreement than disagreement—will work together to make it happen. And time spent worrying, arguing, and being frustrated about relationships is time not being spent on solving the world's problems. Think about it: what could you do for Mankind if you were happy and fulfilled personally?

While I am proud of many things in my life prior to marrying Charley, the fact is that I have accomplished more personal, professional, spiritual, financial, familial, creative, intellectual, charitable, and environmental goals in the 26+ years we've been together, than in all my previous years. Charley will tell you the same thing about himself.

So, after that lengthy preamble, here are some people who helped me along the way:

Mother, for all her faults and personal problems, including alcoholism, prescription drugs, and untold marriages, gave me gifts of immeasurable value: She believed in me. She believed I was good. She believed I was smart and could figure things out. In the end, she was right, even if it took me a while to catch on in the relationship department. Thank you, Mom.

My son Josh and his wife Eve, stepdaughter Amy, stepson Simon, former stepson Adam, and grandkids Diana, Lorelei and Pearl. Oh my gosh, what haven't I learned from them?! Patience. Tolerance. Understanding. Life lessons. They are all smart, bright, creative, talented, and good-hearted people. I am truly blessed.

My brother and sister-in-law, Mark and Barbara Oman, for being inspirations. I couldn't have asked for a better brother, who was my "biggest fan" when he was practically the only one in the club.

My Dad, Paul Oman, for letting me make my own mistakes "almost" without comment. It must have been maddening for him when faced with some of my choices, but whether he believed I would get my head on straight eventually or not—and while he did give his opinions—he pretty much left me alone to figure things out for myself. I don't know if he did that intentionally or not, but the net effect is that I turned out pretty well. Thanks, Dad. (I was able to spend time with Dad on the eve of his passing. I know he's proud of me.)

I am blessed with many friends, some of whom really tried to help me get sorted out during "the dark years." Diana Watson, Stephanie Hamilton, Bill and Joava Good, Yvonne Gillham, Mary Elizabeth Glosup, Grace Marie Haddy. I should have listened to you sooner!

If it weren't abundantly clear by now, many thanks are due my wonderful husband, Charles Alexander Carr (Charley with an "ey"), for being smart and kind and sexy and funny and understanding and gracious and patient, i.e., for being himself. I cannot imagine life without him and hope I don't have to experience a life without him for a very long time. Without Charley, there would be no book.

ABOUT THE AUTHOR

*T*ANII CARR WAS BORN IN PHILADELPHIA AND *raised in Southern California. Her professional background has been* diverse: television production and programming; *writing, public speaking, media and public* relations for non-profits; multimedia curriculum development for corporate clients; and holistic horse care.

After spending decades writing, speaking and otherwise communicating on behalf of her clients, she now turns her attention toward getting out her own messages of hope and help on a variety of subjects including relationships, the subject of this book. She is currently working on a book about her mother called *Mother Wore Pasties*.

CHARLES CARR was a professional photographer for many years before embracing the "art" of software design and development. His company, Benchmark Software, Inc., is in demand creating the wonderful problem of how to provide all the service being asked for.

Surrounded by an assortment of animals, Charley and Tanii live in a small, horsey suburb of Los Angeles called Shadow Hills.

To contact Tanii about her book and related products and services, or just to say "hello!" go to www.10weeks2love.com.